A Spell in the Woods

Stella Wulf

Fair Acre Press

First published in Great Britain in February 2021 by Fair Acre Press

www.fairacrepress.co.uk

ISBN 978-1-911048-50-3

Typeset by Nadia Kingsley

Cover by Claire Jefferson

Acknowledgments

Thank you to the editors of the following magazines in which versions of these poems were first published:

Nightlife, Words for the Wild; *Crow*, Black Light Engine Room; *Spending the Day*, The High Window; *Making Mountains*, Smeuse; *A Spell in the Woods*, and *Pigs Might Fly*, three drops in a cauldron; *Hare Reflects*, The Fat Damsel; *Spring Fever*, London Grip; *The Swan Maiden*, Atrium; *Dream House*, As Above So Below.

Thank you to Nadia Kingsley of Fair Acre Press for giving me the space to bring my loves together and to all those who encouraged me to produce this work – you know who you are, and of course to my lovely husband who smooths out all my technical wrinkles.

About the Author

Claire paints the landscape that is on her doorstep, hence the frequent appearance of mountains, hay bales, and sunflowers, views of which she never tires. She has a deep love of the natural world and a fascination for politics and the human condition – themes that she explores in her poetry which she writes under the pseudonym, Stella Wulf.

Her poems have been widely published and appear in several anthologies including the award winning *#MeToo, The Best of 52, No Spider Harmed,* and *Bloody Amazing.* She was placed third in the *Sentinel Literary Competition 2013,* and nominated for *Best New Poet Anthology 2018.* Journals include: *The New European, London Grip, The French Literary Review, Prole, Rat's Ass Review, Ink Sweat & Tears,* and many others. She has an MA in Creative Writing, from Lancaster University and is co-editor of 4Word Press who published her first pamphlet, *After Eden,* in 2018.

www.stellawulf.com

'Where painting is the poetry of sight, poetry is the painting of insight. An image is an evocation; whether elicited through words or colour, it requires structure, composition, meaning and passion. I strive through my paintings and my poetry to encapsulate those insights, emotions and experiences; ultimately – to unite and connect in the name of art.'

Claire Jefferson/Stella Wulf

Preface

As a child of the 50's, I was fortunate to grow up with a freedom not afforded to other generations. My playground was the woods and meadows where we fished for tadpoles, climbed trees, made dens. We caught insects in jam jars to be studied and later released, knew where to look for nests and to which birds they belonged. The title poem, *A Spell In The Woods*, is about the woodland where I played as a child growing up in Wales. Visiting later as an adult, I couldn't reconcile the transformation. Gone was the farm with its meadows and ponds, gone my beloved woodland. In its place a retail park surrounded by acres of car park tarmac.

Wales was my home for almost 40 years and despite an absence of 20 years, I'm still moved to write about it. If there is an air of nostalgia about *Wales Sings*, it's because it's still very much in my heart. Here at the foot of the Pyrenees in South West France where I live, the ever changing landscape is a constant stimulus for both painting and writing. *Spending the Day* is a celebration of those elements that continue to delight me.

This book is the product of a combined love of writing, and drawing and painting. I am both Claire Jefferson the artist and Stella Wulf the poet (if you'll forgive me for giving myself titles). I have pulled my two selves and my two lives together to bring this little book of nature to life.

For all Earth's creatures great or small,
may we all find balance in her scale

Nightlife

After night's fall when the bruised day dies,
we are unfaithful sleep, minds uncloseted,
skeletons through which the wind sighs.

I am the shoulder on which the night cries,
the furrowed brow, a breast pearled in moonlight.
After night's fall when the bruised day dies,

voles tremble, mice quake, owl's fancy flies,
moon slick as cream robes the limbs of trees,
skeletons through which the wind sighs.

I am the realm that never sleeps, tapetum of eyes,
bristle of whisker, whiff of musk, the dank bite,
after night's fall, when the bruised day dies.

I am the burning holes in a pocket of sky,
a bolt—a halt—the lightning strike on asphalt,
skeletons through which the wind sighs.

We are the foxtrot, moonwalk, shadow-dance prize,
cradles of flesh and bone rocked by chance,
after night's fall when the bruised day dies,
skeletons through which the wind sighs.

Crow

He hammered again this morning,
a sharp gavel rap like a bailiff with a writ,
hell-bent on serving it to the devil
that blackens his name, the upstart
who steals his symmetry,
ruffles him with mockery.

Intent on shattering the myth of himself
as dread clarion, bringer of doom,
he can't see past his adversary
to my room where I lie in bed,
so close I can see myself drawn
in the ink of his eye.

All that lies between his world
and mine is a thin, brittle pane.
He's heralded as icon, legend,
but we're both on the threshold,
he and I, perplexed creatures,
chipping away at ourselves.

Wales Sings

an anthem of scarred valleys, hill's uprisings,
a rock of boats on pitch-and-billow seas,
of moon washed moors and drowsy towns,
broody castles settling on old scores,
opening forgotten doors with the turn of a key.

Hunkered houses smoke to fox's nocturne,
blink in the somnolence of owl's lullaby.
Night burrows deep as moles into earth's seams,
until morning unpicks them with a silver blade,
releasing its song into the dazzling day.

And always a ruckus of rooks hacking
over chimney pots, haggling for all things bright.
And beautiful, these gospels of shafted light,
exalting the plainsong of slate, glancing
through windows clear as chapel bells,
and Myfanwy, rising from the piano,
to wring the hearts of men.

Spending the Day

The day is a bright penny cast
from a generous hand, begging
to be seized, bitten on, invested,
a spit'n-shine day to be counted.

The cockerel struts his assets,
crows about his plucky hens,
laying odds on a daily deposit.
The day unfolds its promise,

appraises the gold of orioles,
the notes of countless birds,
rendered to the tune of a tractor,
tedding the year's growth.

Overhead, copper kites bank,
toss and flip, heads and tails,
speculating on the plunder
spilled from under the mattress

of turned hay, the loosed change
of mice and voles, a jeopardy of adders,
accumulated riches to fatten cats
and line the nests of raptors.

The morning weighs its treasures,
pools its cache of sunlight
on the day's treasure trove,
a fortune that is mine to spend.

Making Mountains

We'm roly-poly piccolo dandies
plushy n palpy as pups
roamin the loam, push'n up sods
with us root'n scoot'n handies.

Worms is us lushess guzzle
prodigious gorgers we'm is
snoutin us squirmy larders
fer us own weight of ums.

We'm traps um in tunnels
tongues um slack wi toxy spit
mashes grit from ums gut in a winkin
gobbles ums glutinous tubicles.

We'm a labour of mouldywarps
minin us own business
shovellin out us galleries
pickin'n lickin, graftin'n tilthin
churnin us hills to orogenies.

A Spell in the Woods

Wych elm, elder, aspen, oak,
badger's hideout, hedgepig's poke.

Dogwood, hawthorn, cherry, birch,
woodpeckers larder, roe deer's church.

Blackthorn, alder, rowan, ash,
blackbird's nest egg, squirrel's stash.

Holly, hornbeam, hazel, yew,
hedgerows, meadows, bird's-eye view.

Chain saw, bulldozer, open sores,
Tesco, Pound World, British Home Stores.

Hare Reflects

Hare saw the immaculate whiteness,
an infinite cosmos without horizon,
blanched to a white so pure,
she absorbed nothing.

Out of nothing raged the universe,
she reflected.

Hare scratched and scraped,
seeking out the purple saxifrage,
the bloomed blueberries and bitter sorrel.
She scoured the rime
resurrecting the shrouded earth.

Hare saw the whiteness, riddled.
She saw Chaos and rejoiced.

She dug deep, punctuating the whiteness
with the bone black humus of time,
until the horizon drew a line
and split infinity.
Hare surveyed her opus.

Out of Chaos springs creation,
she declared.

Spring Fever

A clear head of sky relieved of the throb
of planes, throws off its damp grey cover,
yawns in this new liberation of airways.

Birds infectious with spring fever puff
their chests in full-throated song; the soggy lawn
wheezes under a cough of warm breeze.

A gang of daffodils, oblivious to the whirring scythe
heading their way, paints the roadsides yellow, brazenly
fraternising as if immune to the vagaries of nature,

as if resistant to the chill that kills the frail, the sickly,
the precocious. Tulips stay home, tightlipped in isolation,
strict in conformity, mustering reserves for hard times.

Squirrels, who stashed enough for Winter's siege,
empty the bird feeders, their pouches stuffed
to bursting. It's every beast for himself, survival

of the greediest. Bees are abuzz with this changed
world order, sedulously forming a new waggle dance
to instruct the hive. The queen readies herself -

spring fever stalks, dandelions mark time, temperatures rise.
It takes the breath away, flutters the heart like birds
in the leafless trees, flocking to the seeded air.

The Swan Maiden

I was reared in a cob and straw clutch,
a plot hatched from a jaundiced yolk,
laid in the hollow of her dead belly,
or that's what he told me.
No one wants an ugly duckling, he said.

Pinioned by his needs, I lumbered
to his call. By night I let fly
my bombilations, a trumpeting lament
taken up by the wind, threshing
on a wing chord.

***

A dawning sun rises in my gorge,
sears the salt lakes of my eyes,
beats at my body's cage.

My gut unravels - knots to a skein,
catching my breath in its mesh
as I lift from his battered chest,
a pellicle of white skin and down,
a pleated vane of coverts,
the earthy scent of summer rain,
pulsing a madness through my veins.

Slipping back into the stolen shift,
I open my wings, stretch out my neck,
taste the iron in the spreading pool,
observe my reflection in the slick.
See now, how fair I am?

Pigs Might Fly

He made her a bed from fallen willow,
turned the greenwood of its wedlock head,
pillowed it plump with a bolstered sham.
He sewed her a cover of rough spun yarn,
stitched her in time to his cold comfort farm.

She smarted with the salt of his keeping,
wept buckets of tears at every squealing,
till she and the pigs were steeped in the brine.

The homespun wives came at full moon-shine,
touting black cat tales, concoctions, notions.
She bought their threads a-penny-a-thought,
wove the silks to a web of schemes,
fixed it high in the wishing tree.

He said she could leave when pigs might fly
but she and the pigs wanted earthly things,
some ground to nurture their budding dreams.

She made him a bed under candlewick cover,
a pillow of loam to cradle his head,
rocked him to sleep neath the wishing tree.
There he will lie till the pigs grow wings.

Shooting Beaver

Eager for my first shot of a sleek pelt, I hunker down
in the dank hollow, set my focus on the far bank,
relive the centuries in the waiting.

I marvel at the gnawing obsession that brought us
to this brink - how, in this long chain of events, we ditched
fur for polymer, damned our world with a barrage of waste,
the silt of entitlement, a flood of insouciance.

The whiff of castoreum hooks me with its flesh
and blood promise, I hope for something - anything,
to break the tension, shatter the float glass sky to smithereens.

Nothing stirs, even the sun's patience is waning - it sidles off
through the trees to bed, a watery-eyed somnambulant,
and I'm reminded that tonight a beaver moon will bear down
on our excessive trappings.

But look! The waters break - a head breaches, sculls
the river's cord, towing its newborn days in a purl
of liquid silk. This small creature paddling twilight,

is back to mend our ways, rebuild the centuries
of ruinous acts, restore our errant nature. I shoot -
capture him in the shadow's bars, lock him in
to this snapshot of time.

The Heron's Cup

The priestly cleric stalks
secular haunts - low dives
seedy dykes - watering holes
predatory lust by lustre lured
shivers the pond to ecstasy
pooled gold flicks - rolls
heads or tails?
He preys
silently
reverently
answers the call
bows to the water
takes his communion
tastes blood and body
divine.
Auri
sacra
fames
served
water crossed
the priestly cleric stalks
the potters field and preys
gilt will lure him further out of grace.

Dream House

You pry open the shutters, intruding on a house where time long ago threw up its hands, surrendered to solitude. Raggedy bats string the beams – frayed charms of bombazine. Startled by the brazen trespass of day, they cast off, reel away like dropped stitches, the pattern of their lives unravelling.

A feverish *vent d'autan* wheezes through crannies, skitters up husks, sighs over small carcasses, the bone-dry litter of a spent era. Disturbed, the scurf of the dead rises, circulates through its old haunts. The house yawns, timbers flex, venerable joints creak and crack.

Outside, somewhere, a chainsaw gripes at oak's grain, a plane grumbles over blotted sky, a tractor chunters at clay. Close by, the shock of a flesh and blood snore - something lurks behind the outhouse door, the privy where once hunkered the buttocks of *les ouvriers*, toiling to relieve their lot. Lifting the latch, peering in, you are hit by the scent of hay, lustily overlaid with corporeal musk, a bludgeon to your senses.

Oblivious to his den's past movements, Badger, ball-curled, sleeps in snouting soundness. Nature's child, you snub fate, thumb your nose at unworldly lore, but in the rise and fall of substance, the steady rhythm of a body's core - in this crystal-clear moment, you read your future.

To Phil, my very own eagle-eyed badger,
my prickly hedgehog,
my canny fox, thank you for sustaining
all those white hares I gave you - they're multiplying nicely.